Bright Ideas

FOR

Early Years

Christmas Activities

Susan Godfrey

Contents

Published by Scholastic Publications Ltd,
Villiers House, Clarendon Avenue,
Leamington Spa, Warwickshire CV32 5PR.

© 1990 Scholastic Publications Ltd

Reprinted 1991, 1991

Written by Susan Godfrey
Edited by Jackie Cunningham-Craig
Sub-edited by Catherine Baker
Designed by Sue Limb
Illustrations by Helen Herbert
Front cover artwork by Mary Lack
Photographed by Martin Chillmaid

Artwork by Liz Preece,
Castel Graphics, Kenilworth
Printed in Great Britain by
Loxley Brothers Ltd, Sheffield

British Library Cataloguing in Publication Data
Godfrey, Susan
  Bright ideas for early years.
  Christmas activities
  1. Nursery schools. Teaching
  I. Title
  372.1102

  ISBN 0-590-76298-2

Introduction

The activities in this book have been tried and tested in a nursery group over a period of several years. They can all be adapted for the differing abilities of children from four to six years of age, and may be used in a variety of settings with a range of different materials, depending on what is available.

   These activities will be equally successful in a nursery group or at home. They are fun to do, and should give rise to some interesting teaching opportunities. They can also provide an opportunity to practise language and creative skills in a relaxed and enjoyable way.

The activities are directed to a certain extent, and they should ideally take place within a stimulating environment where free experimentation and expression form the greater part of the child's activities. Skills which young children are acquiring during their free play can be channelled and put to good use in activities which involve producing cards, decorations and gifts.

Obviously only a few of these ideas will be used in any one season, and it may be helpful to keep notes on the use of the activities from year to year. The ideas are not intended to be an end in themselves, but can be adapted and extended in many ways to suit your children and their needs.

Things to collect

It is a good idea to collect bits and pieces throughout the year so that when the Christmas season arrives you are well prepared. The following list covers most of the activities in this book, and can be used as a basis for a collection:

* Seeds (from everlasting flowers, sweet peas, nasturtiums, sunflowers etc),
* Cones (larch are good),
* Silver or gold paper and tinsel,
* Cardboard tubes of varying lengths,
* Pressed flowers, leaves or grasses,
* Wool,
* Odd rolls or books of wallpaper,
* Stickers and toys from crackers,
* Yoghurt or margarine pots,
* Dried lavender, dried herbs,
* Matchboxes,
* Old Christmas paper and cards,
* Parcel string or ribbon,
* Bits from a hole punch,
* Paper plates,
* Cotton wool,
* Sponge,
* Sweet wrappers, foil, milk bottle tops,
* Catalogues and magazines,

- Fabric scraps,
- Candle pieces,
- Eggshells and egg boxes,
- Doilies,
- Round cheese boxes,
- Jam jars,
- Cake cases,
- Straws,
- Toothbrushes (for spatter painting),
- Tiny flower pots,
- Old dishes or picnic bowls.

Notes

Varnishes
PVA adhesive works well as a varnish and is much easier for young children to use than paint varnish.

Pressed flowers
Pressed flowers for pictures can be gathered well in advance. They must be picked fresh and be quite dry. A wallpaper book makes an excellent 'press' providing the papers are not embossed. Sheets of toilet paper help to absorb moisture.

Decorations

Chapter one

It is fun to decorate the room for Christmas, especially if you make your own decorations. The children will need a certain amount of direction, but the activities suggested here involve free use of materials and give scope to the imagination and creative skills. If you provide plenty of spare materials and a little guidance, the children will enjoy experimenting and producing attractive decorations. Working together on the wall murals will involve a great deal of valuable discussion and co-operation.

The tree decorations described here are suitable for all types of Christmas tree. If made in a nursery group they can be taken home and treasured for many years as a decoration for the family tree.

Small decorations

Candles

What you need
Cardboard tubes, white paper, wallpaper, scraps of gold paper, adhesive, crayons or paints.

What to do
Roll the paper round the cardboard tubes, and cut it to fit. It is best to use tubes of several different sizes. Cut flames from the gold paper. Then ask the children to choose a tube and a piece of paper which will fit round it. They can then colour or paint the paper or make a rubbing by placing some embossed wallpaper beneath the white paper, and rubbing with a crayon.

   The children can then stick the decorated paper around the tubes, and add the flames with a spot of adhesive.

Notes
This activity will encourage talk about sizes, shapes, area and length. It can be extended by talking about candles and wax generally. You may like to bring in some real candles, and talk about heat and melting. The children could also play 'Jack be nimble' (see page 65).

Father Christmas mobile

What you need
Paper plates, red paper, cotton wool, egg boxes, sticky paper (or coloured paper and adhesive), paint.

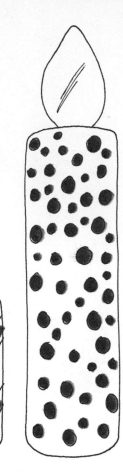
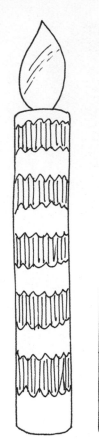

What to do

Cut the red paper into hat shapes. Cut the round parts from egg boxes to make noses. Older children will be able to do this for themselves, and if all the bits are carefully presented, younger children will be able to put together a face of their very own.

The Father Christmas faces look effective hung from the ceiling on a hoop mobile, or as a wall display.

Although the components have been prepared by an adult, each child will use his own imagination and skill in making the faces, and each face will take on its own character!

Paper snowmen

What you need

White paper, coloured paper, pencils, crayons or felt-tipped pens, adhesive.

What to do

Draw a template consisting of one large and one smaller circle, or let the children draw their own. Cut out some hat shapes as well.

Cut round the circles and stick the smaller one on to the larger one as a head. Add the hat, and draw on a face and scarf or buttons.

Notes

Depending on their ability, the children may draw the two circles freehand, draw round two different-sized saucers, trace round two dot-to-dot circles, or use circles which have already been drawn.

This activity can be used to introduce words for shapes and sizes. The children will be able to practise counting with the snowmen, adding up their eyes, noses, buttons and so on.

Printed snowmen

What you need
Circles of foam stuck on to wooden blocks for printing; coloured paper, felt-tipped pens, black sugar paper, white paint.

What to do
Print snowmen using the round foam shapes. Draw their faces with felt-tipped pens, and add a hat. (See 'Printed robins' on page 43 for making printers.)

Snowman picture

What you need
White paper, pencils, scissors, coloured sticky paper, white paint, black sugar paper, adhesive, printers for making snowflakes (you could use potato prints).

What to do
Draw one small and one large circle on the white paper. Cut them out and mount on the black paper in the form of a snowman. Draw on his face, add a hat and print a snowflake pattern around him.

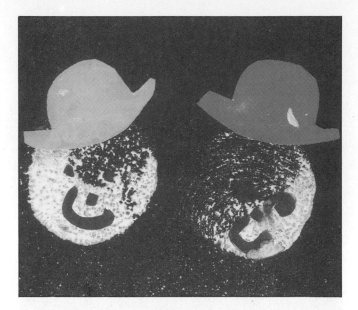

Wax wash snowmen

What you need
Blue or black sugar paper, a candle, white paint, coloured paper, glitter.

What to do
Draw a basic snowman shape on to sugar paper with the candle. (This is too difficult for young children as considerable pressure is needed to make the lines strong enough.) You could add some candle wax snowflakes too.

Ask the children to wash the picture with thin white paint. The wax will resist the paint, and a snowy picture will appear. When the pictures are dry, the children can add hats, glitter and other decorations.

Notes
This is a satisfying activity for younger children, and although the initial shape is prepared for them they can use their skill and imagination in completing the picture.

Hanging decorations

What you need
Card, kitchen foil, a large selection of coloured film and foil sweet wrappers, milk bottle tops, adhesive, cotton or thin parcel string.

What to do
Cut the card into circles and diamond shapes. Cut foil to fit the card shapes, and stick it on to either side of the card. When the shapes are dry, decorate them with a collage of film and foil wrappers. Hang the shapes with cotton or thin parcel string.

Notes
If coloured foil is available you can make colour co-ordinated decorations. This can lead to some interesting discussions about colour!

Paper decorations

What you need
Thin coloured paper or catalogue pages (seed catalogues are probably the most colourful), scissors, felt-tipped pen, adhesive.

What to do
Cut the paper into oblongs about 16cm by 7cm. Fold each piece in half. Draw a guideline for cutting on each piece as shown, using a felt-tipped pen.

Let the children cut the patterns out and open up the shapes. Link the shapes together and secure them with adhesive.

Notes
Older children will be able to fold and cut out their own paper. This activity

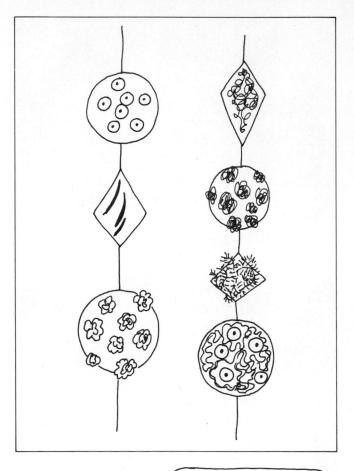

presents a good opportunity for younger children to practise cutting skills using guidelines.

Wall pictures

Christmas card collage

What you need
Old Christmas cards, scissors, paste, cardboard tubes, coloured pens or paint, frieze paper or wallpaper.

What to do
Ask the children to cut round the pictures on the old Christmas cards. When they have a good collection, arrange the pictures closely together and stick them down on a large piece of paper. Leave some overlapping slightly. When the collage is big enough the children can make 'peepers' out of decorated cardboard tubes. It is fun to peep through the tube and find separate pictures on the collage.

Notes
This activity will generate a great deal of discussion while the children choose the pictures to cut out, as they arrange them, and finally as they look at them through the 'peepers'.

Patchwork stocking

What you need
A large piece of strong paper (any colour), scraps of material, cotton wool, adhesive, pictures of toys.

What to do
Cut the scraps of material into small pieces. Draw and cut out a large stocking shape from the paper. Glue the patchwork pieces on to the stocking, covering it completely. Trim the top with cotton wool. Cut out or draw and paint some pictures of toys to tuck into the top of the stocking.

Notes
This is a simple but effective wall decoration. Working together, the children will have a good opportunity to talk about sizes, shapes, colours and textures as the material scraps are selected and used. Talking about presents and painting them will add to the value of this activity.

Carol singers

What you need
Large sheets of strong white paper, black paint, brushes, a pencil, black paper, orange tissue-paper, cotton wool, adhesive, a sunny day or a spotlight!

What to do
Hang up a child-sized piece of paper so that shadows can be projected on to it. Stand a child sideways so that her shadow is central. Draw quickly round the shadow with a pencil, and cut out the shape. Repeat this with several children. They can then paint their own shadows with black paint. Mount the shadows on a large window or wall as carol singers,

grouped around a lantern. The lantern can be cut out of black paper and the spaces filled with orange tissue-paper. Add some cotton wool snowflakes.

Notes
This may sound an ambitious project, but it is worth the trouble. It is surprisingly easy to identify the children by their shadows, and the finished picture will cause much discussion among the children and any visitors who see it!

Houses in the dark

What you need
Black sugar paper, scissors, orange or yellow tissue-paper, white paper, cotton wool, adhesive, white crayon.

What to do
Cut out some house shapes in black paper. If the children are under five it is best to do this for them; they could draw some trees themselves and cut them out. Cut holes in the houses for windows. Carefully put a line of adhesive around the window holes, and cover the holes with scraps of tissue-paper. On a window, make a layer of snow with white paper and arrange the houses and trees on top of this. The light will shine through the tissue-paper windows. For extra effect, add some snowflakes in paint or cotton wool.

Parcel picture

What you need
Bright frieze paper for background, felt-tipped pens, sheets of wrapping paper, flat parcel ribbon or strips of bright paper, scissors, adhesive.

What to do
Cover part of a wall with frieze paper. Draw parcel shapes on the undersides of the wrapping paper. Ask the children to choose a piece of wrapping paper and cut out the parcel shape. They can stick on some ribbon too. Draw a big Christmas tree on the frieze paper and arrange the parcels around it.

Notes
This activity will involve talk about colours, shapes and sizes; it will also give the children practice with cutting skills. Arranging the parcel ribbon and deciding on its length will also provide some good teaching opportunities.

Surprise parcel picture

What you need
White paper, wrapping paper, brightly coloured strips of paper or cheap parcel ribbon, drawings or cut-out pictures of toys.

What to do
Cut the white paper and the wrapping paper into pieces of matching sizes. Use geometrical shapes for variety; they will also help introduce some useful words. Fold the white paper as shown.

Stick the wrapping paper on to the white paper. Draw or stick a picture of a toy under the fold. Add ribbon to the

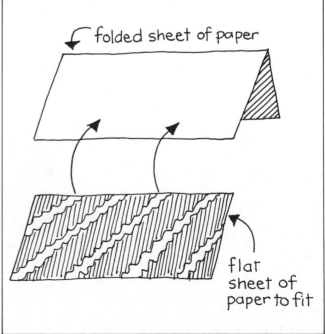

folded sheet of paper

flat sheet of paper to fit

wrapping paper and mount the 'parcel' on the wall.

The children can lift the flaps to see the contents of each parcel. You could complete the picture by adding a Christmas tree and grouping the parcels around it.

Notes
This activity can help the children with shape recognition as well as giving them a chance to improve their general craft skills. It can be adapted according to the children's ages and abilities.

Snowy forest

What you need
Wallpaper books, felt-tipped pens, scissors, white paint, blue frieze paper for background, adhesive, cotton wool.

What to do
Plain white, green or silvery wallpapers are best for this activity. Cut out some fir tree templates, or just draw the shapes and let the children do the cutting out.

Paint a layer of snow along the bottom of the frieze paper. Stick the cut-out fir trees on to the background, and put the final touch to the picture by adding some snowflakes in paint or cotton wool.

Notes
This picture can be used as background for work about cold weather, or you could use it as an illustration for a story.

Shadow shapes

What you need
Black or dark coloured paper, white crayons, thin white paper or tracing paper, adhesive, Blu-Tack.

What to do
Ask the children to choose a Christmassy shape to draw, such as holly, a bell, a star or a snowflake. Use stencils if necessary. Cut out the shapes and mount them on pieces of thin paper. Frame the pictures with strips of card or stiff paper, and stick them on to a window with Blu-Tack.

Notes
This is an interesting and effective activity which can be simple or intricate according to the age of the children.

Talk to the children about light and shadow. Can they see the reason for using different thicknesses of paper?

Cut-out snowmen

What you need
Coloured sticky paper, white paper, scissors, template on page 91.

What to do
Fold the paper as shown, and draw on the snowman outline. Let the children cut round the outline, and unfold the row of snowmen. Then they can colour in the snowmen's faces, and add some buttons, scarves and hats.

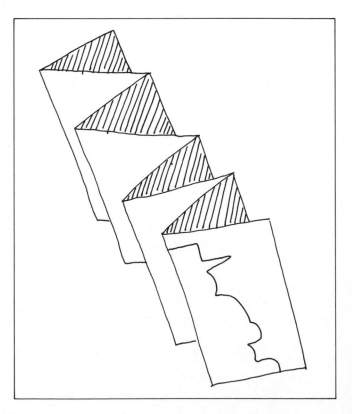

Notes
You could join up the lines of snowmen to make a wall frieze or counting chart.

Tree decorations

Sweet cornets

What you need
White paper, adhesive stick, scissors, wax crayons, pieces of embossed wallpaper, parcel ribbon, a circular template about 16cm in diameter, hole punch, small sweets.

What to do
Place a piece of embossed wallpaper under each sheet of plain paper, and rub the paper with wax crayons to reveal the pattern beneath. Use the template to cut circles from the paper, and fold the circles in half. Cut down the fold. Curve the resulting semicircles into cone shapes and secure with adhesive stick. Punch a hole in each cone, and thread some ribbon through for hanging. Fill the cones with tiny sweets.

Notes
This simple decoration can be varied in many ways. Try trimming the cones with a strip of doily along the curved edge.

   Drawing and cutting the cones can be an interesting mathematical experience. Talk about circles, curves, diameters, halves and semicircles.

Icicles

What you need
Kitchen foil or coloured foil, wool or coloured string, hole punch, pencils.

What to do
Cut the foil into strips about 1.5cm wide and 24cm long. Punch a hole at one end, and make a diagonal cut at the other. Thread loops of string through the holes.

Wind each foil strip along the length of a pencil to make a tube. Slide off carefully. Hang the icicles from the tree by the string loops.

Notes
These are very simple to make, but take care, as they are easily crushed! Make larger icicles for a classroom decoration; they look very attractive hanging from a silver hoop.

Stars

What you need
White, silver, gold or coloured card, star template, adhesive stick, glitter, hole punch, parcel ribbon.

What to do
Draw round the star template and cut out carefully. Colour the star if necessary, and decorate with glitter. Make a hole and add a loop of string or parcel ribbon.

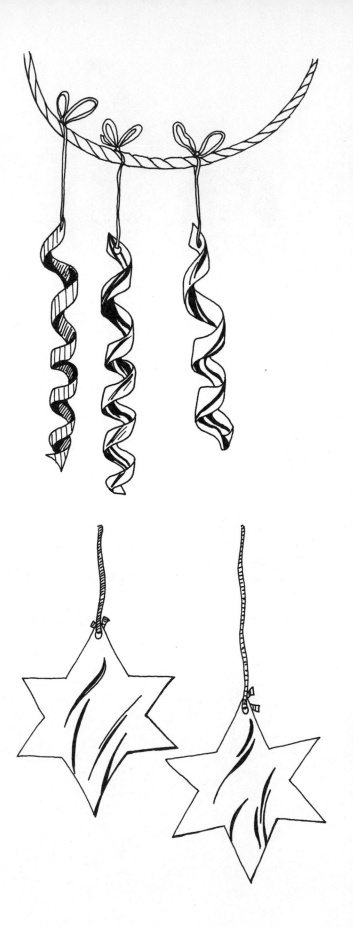

Dough shapes

What you need

Flour, salt, water, rolling pins, *petit four* cutters, thin knitting needle, paint, glitter, parcel ribbon, adhesive.

What to do

Make a dough using three parts flour to one part salt. Add water to make a dough which is pliable but not sticky.

Let the children play with the dough. Roll it and cut out shapes. Make holes in the shapes with a knitting needle. Lay them on trays and dry them in a very low oven until they are hard.

Paint and decorate the shapes, and slip a loop of parcel ribbon through the hole.

Notes

Playing with the dough is probably enough for the younger children, so ask the older ones to cut out several shapes so that the younger ones can join in with the painting.

Eggshells

What you need
Eggshells, ribbon, paint, adhesive, glitter.

What to do
Paint the eggshells, and add glitter. Stick a loop of parcel ribbon on to the top of each eggshell.

Notes
These are tricky to make, as the eggshells are fragile. Talk to the children about fragile things and the need to take special care with them.

Tree-top fairy or angel

What you need
Good quality white paper, scissors, pencils, white, gold or silver doilies, felt-tipped pens, template (see page 92).

What to do
Trace round the template and cut out the patterns. Ask the children to colour the figures, draw their faces and decorate them with pieces of doily. Have a few ready-made examples to show the children.

Tiny robins

What you need
White paper, scissors, template (see page 93), crayons, adhesive stick, parcel string.

What to do
Use the template to draw and cut out the robins. Let the children colour them, stick on their wings and hang them from the tree with thin parcel string.

Notes
You could use cut-out robins from Christmas cards instead of the template.

Snowy cones

What you need
Tiny cones (larch are good), white paint, glitter, strong adhesive, pieces of card, parcel ribbon.

What to do
Paint the cones white and decorate with glitter. Stick two or three in a cluster on a small piece of card. Stick on a bow, and thread a loop of ribbon through the card.

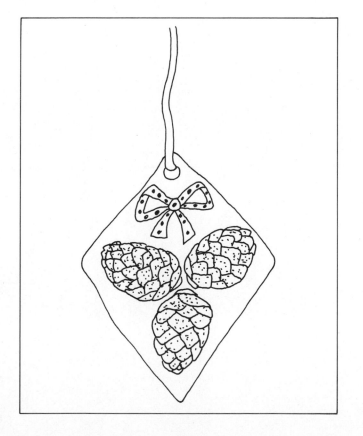

Gifts

Chapter two

Making a small gift for a parent or friend is an important part of the Christmas preparations. This chapter contains ideas for attractive and useful presents which are simple to make.

Each activity can be adapted to suit the age and ability of the children. The gifts are made from materials which are inexpensive to buy, or which are free. It may be useful to look at the 'Things to collect' list on page 6 well in advance, so that you have a few months to collect the necessary bits and pieces.

This chapter also includes suggestions for making 'personalised' wrapping paper, which will add a finishing touch to any home-made present.

Crocus pots

What you need
Yoghurt pots, crocus bulbs, leaf mould, PVA adhesive, scraps of coloured paper or material.

What to do
In order to be ready for Christmas, these pots should be prepared in October.

Ask the children to decorate the pots by sticking on scraps of paper or material. When dry, 'varnish' the pots with PVA adhesive.

When the varnish has dried, fill the pots with leaf mould. Plant and water the bulbs, and store them in a cool, dry place. Bring them into the light and warmth at the end of November.

Notes
Talk about growing plants and the conditions they need. Plant some hyacinths at the same time, and use them for follow-up work in January.

Lavender lady

What you need
Dried lavender, mauve or purple crêpe paper, scraps of parcel ribbon, white card, coloured crayons or pencils, body template (see page 94), adhesive, scissors.

What to do
Cut out rectangles of crêpe paper. Fold them in half and stick the sides together to make pockets.

Use the template to cut doll shapes from the white card. Draw in the dolls' faces, and colour their hair and bodies. Fill the crêpe-paper pockets with lavender, and slip in the dolls so that the lavender bags look like skirts. Stick down

ribbon

lavender bag

firmly, and decorate with ribbon. Stick small crêpe circles on to the backs of the dolls' heads as bonnets.

Notes
This makes a very pretty gift, and the activity can inspire plenty of talk about scents and flowers.

A little seed box

What you need
A matchbox for each child, scraps of pretty paper or material, adhesive, dried flowers, parcel ribbon, flower seeds.

What to do
Cut the paper or material to the right size for covering the matchbox. Write out and photocopy some simple instructions for growing the seeds.

Give the children a box each, and ask them to stick on some material or paper of their choice. Put a few seeds into each box. Put one set of growing instructions into each box, and decorate with dried flowers and ribbon.

Notes
An interesting activity resulting in a simple but useful gift. While covering the boxes there will be an opportunity to talk about shapes and sizes, and filling the box with seeds will promote discussion about seeds and growth.

Read the instructions to the children. By including instructions in the present you will be showing them some of the uses of the written word.

Sunflower

What you need
Round cheese boxes, yellow paper, adhesive, brown paint, sunflower seeds, white paper.

What to do
Paint the base of the boxes with brown paint. Stick circles of white paper over the lids. Cut some petal shapes from the yellow paper, and stick them around the base of the boxes. Place a few sunflower seeds in each box, and put on the lid. Write some simple instructions for growing the seeds on the lids, or write out some more detailed instructions to go inside the boxes.

'Dickory Dock' bookmark

What you need
White or grey card, adhesive stick, crayons, string, template (see page 95).

What to do
Using the template given on page 95, the children can cut out the shapes and stick them together. Colour the clock and the mouse with crayons, and stick on a tail made of cardboard or string.

Notes
This activity can be completed by older children without any help, using the templates and cutting out the shapes themselves. Younger children will need some assistance, but they should be able to assemble the mouse and colour the bookmark.

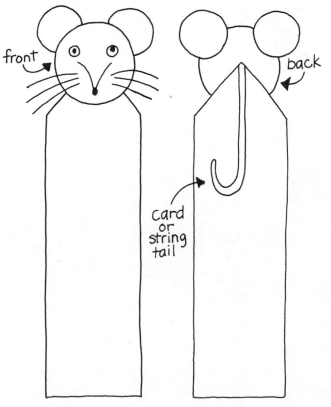

front

back

card or string tail

Recipe folder

What you need
A sheet of thin card or sugar paper, white paper, magazines which have recipes, printers (cotton reels, potato cuts etc), adhesive stick, scissors.

What to do
Cut some pieces of card about 34cm by 28cm. Fold as shown, and stick down the sides to make a pocket folder.

Let the children choose some recipes to slip inside the folders.

Ask the children to help you cut out recipes and pictures of food from the magazines. Print the word RECIPES on pieces of card, and stick one on each folder. The children can decorate the folders with printed patterns and pictures of food.

Notes
This activity results in a useful, attractive present which is very easy to make — even the smallest children can manage it. While making the folders the children will have an opportunity to think and talk about food and cooking.

Reminder board

What you need

Stiff card about 25cm by 17cm, white paper, adhesive, short pencils, string, grey sugar paper, coloured sticky paper, flexible card, wool or ribbon, elephant head templates (see page 96).

What to do

On the grey sugar paper, draw round the elephant head templates. Cut out some eyes from sticky paper. Cut the flexible card in strips 1cm by 5cm.

Ask the children to cut out the shapes you have drawn, assemble them in the shape of an elephant's head and stick them on a piece of stiff card. Staple together some pieces of white paper to make small pads, and stick one on each elephant board. Make pencil-holders with the card strips, or attach the pencils with string. The children can help make a hole in each board with the hole punch, and thread with a loop of ribbon.

Paper flowers

What you need

Cake cases, coloured sticky paper, adhesive, sticky tape, straws.

What to do

Cut circles from the sticky paper to fit inside the bottom of the cake cases. Simply stick a circle into each cake case and attach a straw to the back of each case as a stem. Add some little paper leaves for extra colour; these can also be made from the sticky paper if you wish.

Notes
The flowers will look attractive arranged in a vase. Vases can be made in a variety of ways — cardboard tubes stuck to a card base; covered yoghurt pots weighted with Plasticine; or try making the 'Pretty flower vase' described on page 36.

Sweet dish

What you need
Old dishes or picnic bowls, petroleum jelly, flour and water paste, tissue-paper, thin white paper, last year's Christmas wrapping paper, PVA adhesive.

What to do
Make up the flour and water paste. Smear the outsides of the dishes with petroleum jelly, and cover with tissue-paper. Continue covering the dishes with layers of thin white paper and paste, and finish with a layer of wrapping paper. When the papier mâché is dry, remove the bowls and varnish with PVA adhesive. You will probably need to trim the edges so that they are smooth.

Notes
The completed dish can be filled with sweets on a layer of scrunched-up tissue-paper.

mould paper layers on to dish

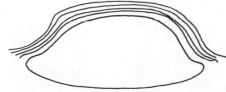

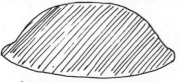
layers stuck on

finished dish

Grow a tree

What you need
Tiny flower pots, potting compost, fir cone seeds, aluminium foil, transparent food wrapping, parcel ribbon, paper, pens, crayons.

What to do
Write out these planting instructions:
- Moisten the compost with water.
- Push the seed under the compost.
- Place in a light position.
- Water gently when the soil looks dry.
- When the seedling is well established, transfer it to a bigger pot.

Add a picture of a tree, and make photocopies. Ask the children to fill each pot with compost, and wrap the seeds in foil, one seed per pot. Then they can colour the tree, and fold up the instructions to place with the wrapped seeds on top of the compost. Cover each pot in transparent film, and add a bow.

Notes
Put a large fir cone in a dry place to open out, and shake out the seeds. There are many seeds in each cone, and they are quick to germinate. The resulting tree may grow to 13cm in a year. If you cannot get fir seeds, use acorns or sycamore seeds.

Watching the tree grow, re-potting it and eventually planting it out is a valuable experience for the children.

Napkin holder

What you need
Small cardboard tubes, crêpe paper or foil, scraps of tinsel, cut-outs from Christmas cards, adhesive stick.

What to do
Cut the cardboard tubes into 3cm lengths. Cut the foil or crêpe paper into strips about 1.5cm wide. Stick the end of a strip to the inside of each piece of tube, and wrap it round and round until the cardboard is covered. Fasten with a dab of adhesive. Decorate with scraps of tinsel or little pictures.

Notes
Napkin rings are not widely used today, but for the Christmas table they can be used to hold paper napkins. You could slip one into each ring as a finishing touch for this present.

Letter rack

What you need
A cereal box, scissors, felt-tipped pen, wallpaper or paint.

What to do
Cut the cereal box as shown in the diagram. (Some children will be able to cut their own if you draw on some guidelines.) Cut wallpaper pieces to fit the sides. Print the word LETTERS on strips of paper, ready for colouring in. Paint the box (it may need two coats) or cover it with wallpaper. Stick the LETTERS label on to the box.

Pretty flower vase

What you need
Jam-jars, newspaper, thin white paper, paints, flour and water paste, PVA adhesive.

What to do
Mix the paste. Tear the newspaper and white paper into tiny pieces, keeping them separate. Ask the children to cover the jars with two layers of newspaper pieces, using plenty of paste. Put a layer of white pieces on top, and leave the jars to dry. Paint them all over with one colour, and leave to dry again. Now the children can decorate the jars with painted patterns, and varnish them with PVA adhesive when they are dry.

Notes
These vases are particularly rewarding to make, as they can be filled with water and used for real flowers.

A little sweet basket

What you need
Thin card, crayons or felt-tipped pens, scissors, hole punch, parcel ribbon, adhesive stick.

What to do
Cut the card into rectangles 11cm by 10cm. Draw 4cm lines in from the corners (see diagram). Colour the card with crayons or felt-tipped pens. Cut along the lines at the corners and fold in the resulting flaps. Stick the edges together and punch holes around the edge. (The children will probably not be able to manage this.) Thread ribbon through the holes and add a ribbon handle. Fill the basket with sweets.

A pretty pomander

What you need
Dried herbs or lavender, or a small bottle of perfume and some cotton wool, thin cotton fabric, thread or strong wool, scraps of ribbon.

What to do
Cut the material into circles about 10cm in diameter, or mark the fabric with guidelines for the children to cut out their own.

Place one or two teaspoons of herbs or lavender in the centre of each circle. Gather up the edges, and tie tightly with wool or thread. Add a ribbon bow. If you have no herbs, use a little ball of cotton wool generously sprayed with perfume.

Notes
As these are easy and cheap to make, the children could make several and pack them in a little box or bag to make an attractive gift.

Candle holder

What you need
Clay (a brand which needs no firing is best), shells or other small objects, paint, PVA adhesive, a candle.

What to do
Give the children time to play with the clay, then give them each a small ball to make into a solid base for a candle. Push a candle half way into the clay ball to make the hole, and gently pull it out. The children can decorate the candle holders by pressing shells and other small objects into the clay to leave a pattern. Leave the holders to dry, and then paint and varnish them. Finally, fit the candles in.

Notes
These candle holders can also be made with plaster of Paris. You could use the bottom of a milk carton or other container as a mould. If you use plaster of Paris you will need to supervise very closely, and although it is fun to use, it dries so quickly that it is not really as satisfying as a good session of free play with the clay!

Wrapping paper

What you need
White paper, paints, assorted printers, trays lined with sponge or kitchen roll to contain the paint.

What to do
Let the children cover sheets of paper with printed patterns.

For an abstract design, use any sort of potato or clay printer. Small pieces of screwed up paper also make good printers. Encourage the children to fill all the space. It may help if you mark the paper lightly with pencil, so that they can make a print on each mark.

You could also try making a design of robins, using sponge printers as described in 'Printed robins' on page 43.

For a holly pattern, make a raised holly template with layers of card cut to shape and stuck on to a wooden printing block. Dip the block in green paint and print the pattern on the paper, adding some berries in red.

Christmas cards

Chapter three

Parents and friends are always pleased to receive a card which has been made for them specially by a child. This chapter contains suggestions for some simple card designs which are intended to stimulate the imagination; both you and the children will probably come up with some additional ideas.

Some children will probably be able to write their own greetings, but you can help the others by drawing letter outlines for them to trace, or giving them letter stamps to print with.

Snowman card

What you need
Coloured card, scissors, adhesive, white paper, cotton wool, sticky paper, narrow strips of cloth or thick wool, hole punch, crayons.

What to do
Cut out one large and one small circle from a piece of white paper. Assemble as a snowman on the front of a folded piece of card. Draw in a face and hat, or use sticky paper shapes. Punch two holes where the head and body join, and thread through a strip of cloth or wool to be a scarf. Tie the scarf in a knot.

Sheep on the hills

What you need
Blue card, white paint, black felt-tipped pen, black paper, white paper, cotton wool, glitter.

What to do
Fold and cut the blue card, and paint on a base of snow. Cut some sheep's head and body shapes from the black and white paper, or use blobs of cotton wool for the sheep's bodies. Stick the sheep on the card, and draw on their legs with a black pen. Add some snowflakes and glitter as a finishing touch.

Notes
While making this card, you could build the whole session round sheep, their wool, and warm woollen clothes.

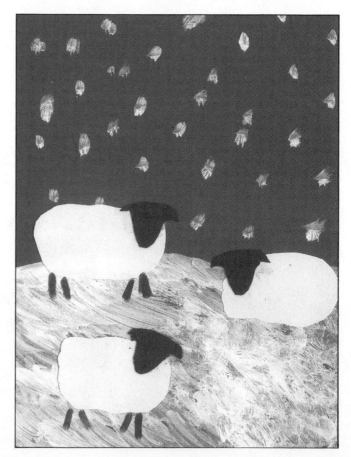

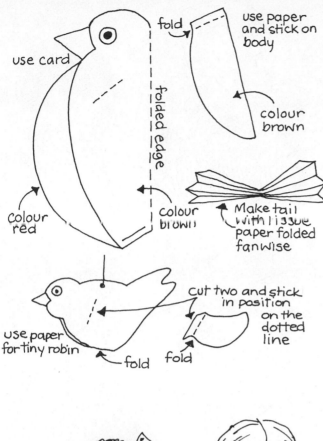

use card

fold

use paper and stick on body

colour brown

folded edge

colour red

colour brown

Make tail with tissue paper folded fanwise

use paper for tiny robin

fold

fold

cut two and stick in position on the dotted line

Robins

What you need
Thin white card or thick paper about 20cm by 24cm, adhesive, crayons, brown tissue-paper, white paper, robin template (see page 93).

What to do
Using the template, cut the shapes from the white card, and fold the robin's body into shape. Cut and fold the tissue paper 'tails' as in the diagram (you may have to help younger children with this). Colour the robin and his wings, and stick the wings into position. Slip the tail through the slit and secure it with a dab of adhesive. Finally, fan out the tail.

Christmas tree

What you need
A wallpaper book, pencils, scissors, adhesive or wallpaper paste, dark coloured card, coloured sticky paper, white paint, glitter.

What to do
Let the children choose some pieces of wallpaper; silvery, pale green or fern-patterned ones are best. Then they can draw some tree shapes on the back, using a template if necessary. Cut out the shapes and stick each tree on to a card base. Add a pot for each tree, and paint on some snow. Decorate with glitter.

Notes
This is a very simple but effective card that can be varied in several ways. The tree templates could be varied in size, or several small trees could be grouped together.

An unusual cracker card

What you need
Pieces of card about 17cm by 7cm, folded lengthways, crêpe or tissue-paper, felt-tipped pens, foil strips, scraps of tinsel.

What to do
Cut the folded cards into cracker shapes. Cut foil strips to fit across the centre, and stick crêpe frills on to the ends. When you have prepared the basic cracker shape, the children can draw or paint patterns on the crackers, and stick the foil and tinsel scraps across the middle.

Notes
Because of the trims on either end, this card stands on its long side. Some children will be able to make the cards with little assistance, but others will need help with the preparation.

Printed robins

What you need
Pieces of foam, cotton reels of different diameters, latex adhesive such as Copydex, a piece of sponge, a dish for the paint, red crayon, felt-tipped pens, brown and white paint, card.

What to do
Make small and large circular printers by sticking circles of foam to the ends of cotton reels with the latex adhesive. Leave to dry. Put the sponge into the dish and soak with brown paint to make a printing pad.

On a card base, print a large circle for the robin's body and a smaller one for the head. Draw a simple beak and some legs with felt-tipped pens. When the robin is dry, use the crayon to give him a red breast. Add some grass or snow, and paint or stick on some snowflakes.

Notes
Although these cards require a certain amount of preparation, they are very effective and easy to make. The children's own individuality and imagination will shine through, even though they are all using the same basic shape!

Holly leaves

What you need
Stiff card, thin card, thin white paper, glitter, wax crayons, adhesive stick.

What to do
Make a raised pattern for rubbing by drawing holly leaves on thin card, cutting them out and mounting them on pieces of stiff card. Leave them to dry. Make several of these for the children, varying the arrangement of the leaves.

Ask the children to make rubbings by placing the prepared cards beneath a piece of thin paper and rubbing with a wax crayon. Mount the resulting pictures on card bases using the adhesive stick, and decorate the cards with green or gold glitter.

Notes
This is a satisfying activity, as the children can play with the rubbing cards and experiment with various colours before choosing the best result to use for the card.

Candle card

What you need
Pieces of embossed wallpaper, pencils, wax crayons, adhesive, foil, glitter, card, thin white paper.

What to do
Make some raised templates for wax rubbing — cut candle shapes from the wallpaper and stick them on card bases.

Let the children make rubbings with coloured crayons, so that the candle picture appears on the paper. Give them time to experiment. Mount each child's chosen rubbing on a card, and let them

add a foil flame and decorate the candle with glitter.

Notes
The embossed wallpaper gives the candles an attractive pattern. Adapt this idea for use with other shapes; the children could make their own templates for rubbing. A collage of wallpaper pieces makes an interesting surface for rubbings.

A pretty Christmas tree

What you need
Coloured card, green sugar paper, a tray of coloured bits collected from a hole punch machine, adhesive, glitter, paper towels.

What to do
Draw and cut out individual Christmas tree shapes to fit the cards. (Younger children may need help.) Carefully stick a tree on each card. Dot the trees with adhesive, and shake the coloured paper bits on to the cards. Cover with paper towels, and press down. Shake the loose pieces back into the tray. Add some glitter.

Notes
If you can collect a whole tray of white paper spots, you could add some snow falling gently around the tree!

Spatter paint designs

What you need
Coloured card, stencils or pressed leaves, paint, old toothbrushes (or a can of spray paint).

What to do
Ask the children to place a stencil or a pressed leaf on their card. Then they can dip a toothbrush in paint, and hold it, bristles down, over the stencil. Spray the paint on to the card by rubbing a finger across the bristles. Hold the stencil still, and keep spraying until the card is nicely covered. Remove the stencil and leave the picture to dry. Of course, you can achieve the same effect by using a can of spray paint instead.

Notes
Spatter-painting is great fun, so give the children plenty of time to experiment freely before they make the cards. Aprons with sleeves are essential, and stand by with a flannel! Canned spray paint is easier to control, but it does cost more and the range of colours is likely to be limited.

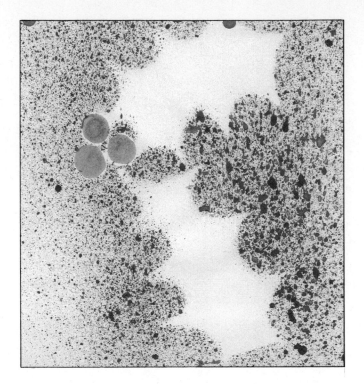

Letter card

What you need
White paper, a silver or gold pen, adhesive stick, pieces of card about 20cm by 16cm.

What to do
Fold the cards lengthwise. Print the letters 'HAPPY CHRISTMAS' on pieces of white paper and cut them up. Make one set per child. Each child can then try to sort the letters into the correct order; make an example card to help. When they have tried this they can mount the letters on the

cards using the adhesive stick, and decorate the edges of the cards with glitter or pens.

Notes
This is an interesting activity which encourages letter recognition. It also results in a very attractive card.

Calendars

Chapter four

A calendar is an inexpensive and useful gift, and making one gives plenty of scope for craft skills.

The following ideas and suggestions have deliberately been kept basic, and they can easily be expanded with your own ideas and the children's suggestions.

Don't forget to choose a picture which will be nice to look at all year round — you probably won't want to be confronted with Christmas trees in the middle of July! With older children you could make four pictures, one for each season, and put them together as a 'turn-over' calendar.

It may help to start accumulating pictures and materials in advance; refer to 'Things to collect' on page 6.

To make any calendar you will need a little stick-on calendar book, which can be bought quite cheaply.

Vase of flowers

What you need
Calendar books, card, wallpaper, white paper, crayons, tissue-paper, green and brown felt-tipped pen, adhesive stick.

What to do
Cut flowers from the tissue-paper, using lots of colours. Cut vase shapes from the white paper, and cut a strip of wallpaper to fit the base of the card.

Let the children stick the wallpaper strip along the bottom of the picture. Then they can colour the vase, and stick it on top of the wallpaper strip. Let them draw stems for the flowers, and stick on the flower heads with a dab of adhesive. (The flowers are easy to pick up with a dampened fingertip.) Finally, stick on the calendar book.

Notes
Several skills are needed to assemble the picture. Older children should be able to make this from paper scraps, with just the tissue-paper flowers prepared for them.

Pressed flower picture

What you need
Pressed flowers, paper leaves, vase templates, card, crayons, adhesive, calendar books.

What to do
Prepare some vase templates in advance, and cut out some paper leaves. The children can choose a vase template and draw round it on a piece of card. Then they can colour the vase, draw some stalks and stick on the leaves. Next, add the dried flowers with a dab of adhesive, and finally stick on a calendar book.

48

Calendar

Notes

Daisies are good for this picture; they are very widely available and can be collected and pressed during the summer without fear of endangering the species!

Daisies are also fairly easy to handle, and they make a very attractive picture — the more flowers the better. If you prefer, the picture could show a field full of daisies instead of a vase.

This can be an interesting follow-up to a summer activity. Making the picture will involve pencil skills, colouring and arranging, as well as counting and sharing the daisies.

Cat calendar

What you need

Black sugar paper, green paper, white paper, calendar books, paper-fasteners, adhesive stick.

What to do

With the black paper, make some cat shapes as illustrated. You may have to cut them out for young children, but older ones will be able to cut round an outline, or even draw their own.

Stick the parts of the cat together, and use a paper-fastener to secure the tail. Add some green paper eyes and white whiskers, and stick on a calendar book.

Notes

If you have no black paper, use white and just colour the cat in. An ideal activity for adapting to different age groups.

Calendar

Leaf print

What you need
Leaves, foam squares set in trays, paint, paper towels, card for mounting, calendar books.

What to do
Press the leaves overnight in a big book. Soak the foam squares with paint.
  Lay the leaves against the foam, vein side down. Let the children press the leaves gently until the back of each leaf is coated with paint. Carefully lay the leaves paint side down on clean white paper, and cover with kitchen towel. Press down, then peel away both towel and leaf to reveal the print. Let the children make several prints, and choose the best ones to mount as calendars.

Notes
Make some printing boards to make pressing down on the leaves easier. Cut a piece of plywood about 12cm by 16cm with a block glued to the centre for a handle.

Leaf rubbing

What you need
Pressed leaves or grasses, thick wax crayons, paper, card for mounting, calendar books.

What to do
Lay the leaves vein side uppermost, and cover with paper. Let the children rub the paper firmly with the side of the crayon, to bring out the pattern of the leaves or grasses. Let the children make lots of these rubbings, and select the best for the calendars.

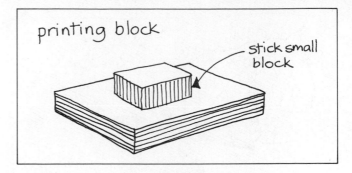

printing block

stick small block

Calendar

Collage calendars

What you need
Scraps of material, paper, seeds, pasta, shells, adhesive, card, pencils, felt-tipped pens, calendar books.

What to do
Let the children choose a basic shape for their calendar, and trace it or draw it freehand on card. They can draw over the outline in thick felt-tipped pen, and then fill the shape with collage. As a finishing touch, decorate the borders of the card too.

Notes
Use very simple shapes for this activity — fishes, flowers, animals and so on. Coloured scraps of paper from magazines look effective, and newsprint on a black background can also be very successful.

Potato prints

What you need
Strong white paper, paints, calendar books, potatoes cut in half to make printers.

What to do
Cut some of the potato printers into specific shapes, and let the children make lots of prints.

After plenty of free play and experimentation, let the children make some calendar pictures with the printers. You might cut the paper into attractive shapes, or use a mixture of printing and collage or painting. Make the prints on strong white paper, cut it to shape and add calendar books.

Sailing boat calendar

What you need
White or pale blue stiff card about 20cm by 15cm, coloured sugar paper, felt-tipped pens or crayons, adhesive, hole punch, calendar books, ribbon.

What to do
Make boat shapes using the coloured sugar paper (see illustration). You may need to cut out the shapes for very young children, but older children could cut round outlines or even draw their own shapes, perhaps using templates.

Assemble the picture on stiff card as shown. Punch some holes in the card, and thread with ribbon for hanging. Stick on the calendar book.

Notes
This calendar is very attractive and simple to make. Even if the shapes are cut out for the children, every picture will be different.

Seasonal calendar

What you need
Four pieces of coloured card per child, hole punch, white paper, thick felt-tipped pens, calendar books, ribbon for hanging.

What to do
During the weeks before Christmas ask the children to make four pictures, one for each season. You could use some ideas from this book, such as a vase of flowers, a daisy picture, a leaf rubbing and a snowman.

Leave a space at the bottom of the picture to print the name of the season — give the children written examples to copy if necessary. Then thread some

ribbon through all four pictures, and attach a calendar by a ribbon loop to the back picture (Winter), so that it hangs just below.

Notes
This more complex calendar provides plenty of opportunity for free craft work and imaginative pictures. It is a very worthwhile project, with opportunities to talk about the seasons and decide on a picture, as well as doing some writing!

Christmas cookery

Chapter five

The Christmas preparations provide some good opportunities for a cookery session. The children could give the food they make as presents, or eat it themselves at a party!

It is generally best to work with a few children at a time while cooking. All the recipes given here have been tested by teachers working with young children, with excellent results.

These activities can give children invaluable experience with weighing, sorting, counting and comparing. There are also lots of new words to learn while the children are dealing with the different ingredients.

Christmas pudding

Making a Christmas pudding at school is not as difficult as it sounds. It can be a rewarding experience educationally, and possibly also financially!

With so many excellent ready-made Christmas puddings available, it is perhaps inevitable that fewer families now make their own puddings. Making one together can be interesting and rewarding for the children. Older ones will enjoy sorting and weighing the ingredients, but with younger children it is best to prepare these in advance. Talking about and handling the ingredients will result in plenty of valuable experience.

The list of ingredients may seem horrendous, but do not worry — you simply mix everything together, and you can do the boiling either at home or in school. Cooking the pudding in school is probably best, as the children can come and check on it regularly.

As for the financial side — if you make the pudding in school, you could raffle it to pay for the ingredients. There might be some money left over to contribute to a party for the children.

The following recipe makes one large and one small pudding — one to raffle and one for the children to try!

What you need

Ingredients: 350g fresh white breadcrumbs, 350g plain flour, one level tsp salt, ½ level tsp ground mace, ½ level tsp ground ginger, ½ level tsp ground nutmeg, ½ level tsp ground cinnamon, 350g shredded suet, 225g caster sugar, 225g soft brown sugar, 175g mixed peel or glacé cherries finely chopped, 275g currants, 225g sultanas, 450g seedless raisins, 175g almonds (chopped or ground), 225g apple (peeled and chopped), grated rind and juice of 1 lemon, grated rind and juice of

1 orange, 3 large eggs (beaten), 150ml milk, 4 tbsp brandy (or extra milk — you may need the brandy yourself!).
Equipment: mixing bowl, small and large pudding bowls, wooden spoons, greaseproof paper, string, saucepans.

What to do

Mix together all the dry ingredients. Mix the fruit juices and rinds with the beaten eggs, and add to the bowl. Add sufficient milk and/or brandy to give a soft dropping consistency. Mix thoroughly, and take turns to make a wish!

Cover the mixture and let it stand. Next day, grease one large and one small basin. Spoon in the mixture, and cover the bowls with greased greaseproof paper. Secure with string.

Adults only — fill two saucepans with boiling water to a level half-way up the pudding bowls, and stand the bowls in the water. Cover the pans and steam for six hours, adding more boiling water if it starts to evaporate. Let the puddings cool, then cover them with fresh paper and store in a cool place.

Shaped biscuits

What you need

Ingredients: 125g plain flour, a pinch of salt, 75g margarine, 75g sugar, an egg.
Equipment: pastry cutters, bowls, rolling pins, baking tray, wooden skewer.

What to do

Rub the margarine into the flour and salt. Add the sugar. Mix to a fairly stiff paste with the egg, adding water if necessary. Roll out the mixture, and cut into festive shapes. Place on a greased baking tray. Press a hole in each biscuit using a wooden skewer. Bake at Gas Mark 4/ 350°F/180°C, until firm and slightly coloured. When the biscuits are cool, ice them (see Iced biscuits, page 58). Thread a piece of ribbon through the holes if you want to hang them from the tree. If you just want to eat them, omit the holes!

Party sandwiches

What you need

Ingredients: sliced bread, spreading margarine or butter, a range of fillings.
Equipment: transparent food wrapping, blunt knives, sticky labels.

What to do

This is an activity for the day of the party! Discuss the party with the children, and present them with a selection of possible sandwich fillings — cheese, egg, peanut butter, jam and so on. Talk about the different tastes.

Let the children take turns to butter, spread and cut their own sandwiches, using the filling of their choice. One slice folded over and cut in two should be enough for pre-school children.

Wrap the sandwiches in the food

wrapping, and label with the children's names. Store the sandwiches somewhere cool until party time.

Notes
Older children will be able to write their own labels, and sort the sandwiches out by matching or reading the names.

This seems a very simple activity, but it will involve a number of teaching opportunities. Children will be discussing the fillings and flavours, as well as spreading and cutting the bread, which demands concentration. There is even some maths work involved in cutting the bread into halves and quarters!

Peppermints

What you need
Ingredients: 400g sweetened condensed milk, 2 tsp peppermint essence, 12 drops green food colouring, 700–900g icing sugar, a few walnuts or pecan nuts.
Equipment: mixing bowl, pastry boards, rolling pins, *petit four* cutters.

What to do
Add the peppermint essence and food colouring to the condensed milk. Stir in 700g of icing sugar. Knead more sugar in, until the texture is firm and smooth. Give each child a small ball to roll out and cut with a *petit four* cutter. Top each sweet with a nut, and leave to dry for at least an hour.

Notes
Let the children help with the measuring and mixing, but you may prefer to do the kneading yourself, as it is quite tricky to get the mixture to the right consistency. You could use the sweets to fill a sweet basket — see page 36.

Iced biscuits

What you need
Ingredients: a packet of plain biscuits, icing sugar, water, two different food colourings.
Equipment: two or three icing sets, a sieve, spoons, two mixing bowls.

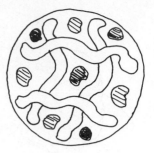

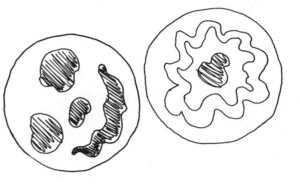

What to do
Sieve the icing sugar, and divide it between two bowls. Add sufficient water to make a thin icing. Add a different food colouring to each bowl. Using the icing nozzles, let the children decorate their own biscuits for the party.

Chocolate dips

What you need
Ingredients: 175g plain flour, 50g caster sugar, 100g margarine, 100g chocolate, vanilla essence.
Equipment: mixing bowl, saucepan, baking trays, fork, cup.

What to do
Rub the margarine into the flour, and add the sugar and vanilla essence. Knead and squeeze the mixture into a firm ball. Divide the mixture into 12 balls. Put them on a baking tray, and press gently with a fork. Bake at Gas Mark 5/375°F/190°C for 20 minutes. When the biscuits are cool, melt the chocolate in a cup over hot water. Dip the biscuits in the chocolate and leave them to dry.

Notes
This simple recipe is very successful with small children. The more the mixture is squeezed the better the biscuits are!

The children will obviously need careful one-to-one supervision when they are dipping the biscuits. If this is not

possible, don't worry; the biscuits are very good without the chocolate!

Cheesy shapes

What you need
Ingredients: 125g plain flour, ¼ tsp salt, 75g grated cheese, 75g margarine, an egg.
Equipment: mixing bowl, spoons, rolling pins, *petit four* cutters, baking trays.

What to do
Rub the margarine into the flour and salt. Add the grated cheese. Mix to a stiff paste with the egg, adding water if necessary. Roll out thinly and cut into shapes. Bake on a greased baking tray at Gas Mark 4/350°F/180°C, until firm and slightly coloured.

Crispy cakes

What you need
Ingredients: 12 tbsps cornflakes or rice cereal, 50g margarine, 2 tbsps golden syrup, 4 tbsps drinking chocolate, silver cake decorations.
Equipment: saucepan, spoons, cake cases.

What to do
Melt the margarine and golden syrup, and stir in the chocolate and cornflakes. Spoon the mixture into cake cases, and leave to set. Decorate the cakes with silver balls for a Christmassy effect.

Notes
If you make some tiny cakes, you can use them to fill a sweet basket – see page 36.

Sugar mice

What you need
Ingredients: 450g icing sugar, water to mix, glycerine or cooking oil, colouring, a few split almonds and currants, strings of liquorice.
Equipment: sieve, mixing bowl, card.

What to do
Sieve the icing sugar, and add a few drops of glycerine or oil. Slowly mix in enough water to form a very stiff paste. Let the children shape small balls of the mixture into mice. Put each mouse on a piece of card, and add almond ears, currant eyes and liquorice tails. Write the children's names on the cards.

Notes
These mice can be wrapped in transparent film and hung on the Christmas tree, or used to decorate name cards at a party. They also make a nice present.

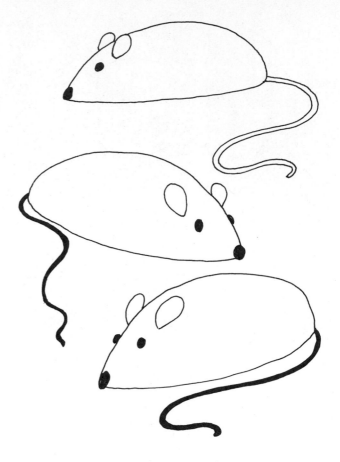

Coconut squares

What you need
Ingredients: 450g icing sugar, 225g desiccated coconut, 6 tbsps condensed milk, pink food colouring.
Equipment: bowls, spoons, spatula, small rectangular baking tin.

What to do
Mix the sugar and coconut with the condensed milk, and divide the mixture into two bowls. Colour one bowlful pink. Dust the tin with icing sugar, and press in the mixture, one colour at each end. Mark into squares and leave to set.

The party

Chapter six

This chapter includes ideas for food, games, songs and things to make for a traditional Christmas party. The children will enjoy helping with the preparations, and everything they produce will help make the party a special occasion. The excitement, anticipation and enthusiasm will all increase as the day of the party approaches, and some excellent teaching opportunities can arise in this atmosphere.

The following activities give scope for a great many skills, and will also encourage language development.

In these as in all other directed activities, the children should be free to experiment and play with the materials, bringing in their own imagination and ideas.

Frilly place mats

What you need
Sheets of paper about 25cm by 20cm, pictures cut from Christmas cards, wax crayons, waterproof felt-tipped pen, embossed wallpaper pieces the same size as the paper, adhesive stick, scissors.

What to do
In advance, draw some lines at either end of the sheets of paper for the children to cut into frills. Place a piece of wallpaper under each sheet, and let the children rub the paper with the wax crayons to reveal the pattern. Then they can cut the frills, using the guidelines. Finally, they can stick on a picture, and write or copy their names.

Cup and plate mats

What you need
Pieces of paper about 25cm by 20cm, paper plates and cups, pencils, crayons, waterproof felt-tipped pens, adhesive, pictures cut from Christmas cards.

What to do
Place a paper plate upside down on each paper mat, and draw round it with pencil. Draw round the paper cup in the same way. Let the children go over the pencil lines with felt-tipped pen, and colour the plate and cup shapes. Finish the mats by adding a picture and the children's names.

Crowns

What you need
Strong paper or thin card, felt-tipped pens, scissors, adhesive, bright-coloured scraps for collage.

What to do
Cut the paper into strips about 9cm by 60cm. Draw crown patterns on the strips as illustrated. Let the children cut out the pattern, and decorate the crowns with collage. Stick the ends together to fit the children's heads, and write the owner's name inside each crown.

Notes
Given a free hand and plenty of collage bits, the children will be able to cover the basic crown shape with some very individual decorations. Older children will be able to draw their own crown patterns using a template made from strong card. These templates are also useful for pre-writing practice.

Party food

Ideas for making party food can be found in 'Christmas cookery' — see pages 53 to 60. Other goodies that are very popular include hot dogs, tiny cakes, marshmallows, chocolate biscuits and crisps. Keep the food very simple, so that any leftovers can easily be taken home or kept for another day.

Games

A detailed list of games has been included as it is easy to forget the traditional games. A short description of each game has been given, although many will already be familiar. Of course, all these games could be played at any time of year.

Musical bumps

Tape some bouncy music in advance. Ask the children to dance around to the music, and when it stops the last one to sit down is 'out'. With very small children there is no need to be 'out' — just bump down for the fun of it!

Pass the parcel

This is an old favourite, and there is no need for detailed instructions, but here are two pointers for success:
- If you are dealing with large numbers sit the children in groups, with one parcel to each group.
- Make sure that the surprise is wrapped in layers which come off easily!

I sent a letter to my love

Ask the children to stand in a circle, singing:

'I sent a letter to my love
And on the way I dropped it
Someone must have picked it up
And put it in their pocket.'

One child walks around the outside of the circle holding an envelope, and chanting: 'It wasn't you, it wasn't you, it wasn't you . . .' Then he drops it behind one of the other children, who turns, picks up the letter and chases the first child once around the circle. Then the second child has a go at dropping the letter, and so on.

Sandy girl (or boy)

One child sits in the middle of the room, pretending to cry. The others join hands around her and walk in a circle, singing:

'Here's a little sandy girl
Sitting on a stone
Weeping, crying, all the day alone.
Stand up sandy girl,
Dry your tears away,
Choose the one you love the best
And then run away!'

At this the child in the middle chooses another child, and they chase around the circle and back to the space. Then the chosen child becomes the sandy boy or girl, and so on.

Looby Loo

All the children dance round in a circle, singing:

'Here we go Looby Loo,
Here we go Looby Light,
Here we go Looby Loo,
All on a Saturday night'.

Then they stand still to sing the following verse and do the actions:

'You put your right foot in,
You put your right foot out.
You shake it a little
And you turn yourself about.'

Sing this verse four more times, putting your left foot, right hands, left hands and then finally your whole selves in! Finish by singing the 'Looby Loo' verse again.

Jack be nimble

'Jack be nimble
Jack be quick
Jack jump over the candlestick!'

Ask the children to sit in a circle. Build a 'candlestick' in the middle, using cylindrical bricks or a cardboard tube. As the rhyme is said, the children take turns to jump over the candlestick.

It's fun to substitute the children's names for Jack's in the rhyme. Make sure the candlestick is at a suitable height for the children to jump over!

A princess lived in a big high tower

Choose children to be a princess, a wicked witch and a prince. Everyone joins hands and sings:

- 'A princess lived in a big high tower,
  A big high tower, a big high tower,
  A princess lived in a big high tower
  Long, long ago.
- A wicked witch she cast a spell,
  Cast a spell, cast a spell . . .
- She fell asleep for a hundred
  years . . .
- A big tall forest grew around . . .
- A handsome prince came galloping
  by . . .
- He cut those trees down with his
  sword . . .
- He woke the princess with a kiss . . .
- So everybody's happy now . . .'

As the children are singing, the following actions are performed:

- The princess stands in the middle of the ring. The children join hands around her, and hold them high to make the tower.
- The witch waves her arm over the princess and runs away.
- The princess lies down and shuts her eyes.
- The children stretch up and wave their arms like trees.
- The prince gallops round the circle.
- He pretends to cut down the trees, and the children sit down.
- He goes into the circle and wakes the princess.
- The prince and princess skip round holding hands while the children clap.

   Using props like crowns, a sword and a witch's hat can make this game even more fun.

Hoops

Spread some hoops over the play area, one per child. Ask each child to stand in a hoop. When the music starts they dance among the hoops, and when it stops they quickly find a hoop to stand in. Remove the hoops gradually, so that any child left without a hoop is 'out'.

Mr Bear

'Isn't it funny
How a bear likes honey?
Buzz, Buzz, Buzz.
I wonder why he does.
Go to sleep, Mr Bear (pause)
Wake up, Mr Bear,
Someone's stolen your honey pot!'

The children sit in a circle. One child is Mr Bear, 'sleeping' in the middle of the circle with his honey pot. Meanwhile, the other children say the rhyme. During the pause one child creeps up and takes the pot, and goes back to the circle, hiding it behind his back. Then all the children call, 'Wake up, Mr Bear!' Mr Bear tries to guess who has the pot. When he has found out, the child who was hiding the pot becomes the next Mr Bear. If the children are very quiet, Mr Bear can listen for footsteps!

67

Songs and rhymes

Christmas songs and rhymes are an essential part of the traditional celebrations. There is a great deal of enjoyment to be had from singing songs together, and children can find it very rewarding to learn the words and tunes and sing along with the others. Singing together can give the children valuable experience of what it is like to join in with other people and create something.

The children will enjoy singing their favourite songs at a Christmas party. Songs can add a certain sparkle and excitement to the pre-Christmas atmosphere, but you can also use a slow, gentle song to quieten things down if the atmosphere gets *too* exciting!

Use Christmas songs and rhymes to add variety to assemblies and plays. Songs can also add to the enjoyment of creative activities. It can be fun for the children to sing as they work at making something — if they are making a robin card, for example, you could find a song about a robin for them to sing. Encourage impromptu singing sessions, too. The possibilities are endless!

The following list contains the titles of some books which you may find useful when choosing songs and rhymes for Christmas. In addition to those books which deal specifically with seasonal songs, we have also listed some of the more general rhyme collections aimed at very small children, which can also be a good source of entertaining and relevant rhymes.

Christmas songbooks

Carol, Gaily Carol
Beatrice Harrop (A&C Black)

Christmas Songs
(Ladybird)

Christmas Things to Sing
Pat Smith and Dorothy Wheatley (EJ Arnold)

Christmas Tinderbox
Sue Nicholls (A&C Black)

Kingfisher Christmas Book
(Kingfisher)

Sing Nowell!
Timothy Roberts and Jan Betts (A&C Black)

Sing-Song-Roundabout Christmas
Brenda Piper and Frank Cooke (Longman)

This Little Puffin . . .
Elizabeth Matterson (Puffin)

Walker Book of Read-aloud Rhymes for the Very Young
Jack Prelutsky (Walker)

Young Puffin Book of Verse
Barbara Ireson (Puffin).

Assemblies

Chapter seven

A Christmas assembly can be presented in many ways, but whatever you choose, the most important thing will be the joyous atmosphere. Playing a part, however small, is a very important experience for the children.

This chapter includes ideas for assemblies which can easily be adapted. Keep costumes simple — children love to dress up but cannot cope with fiddly or restrictive costumes. Avoid using masks; they muffle the voice, and can frighten some children.

Christmas joy

What you need

A tape of quiet introductory music, a cardboard 'door' with a light behind it, a Christmas crib, a small Christmas tree, cards with large letters spelling out the words CHRISTMAS JOY.

What to do

The basic idea for this assembly is to spell out the words CHRISTMAS JOY while illustrating different aspects of Christmas. Cut the twelve letters from paper, and mount them on card. Make or improvise an 'inn door'. If possible, arrange a light behind it which can be switched on.

Choose children to take the individual parts, and arrange a screen for them to stand behind. Set up twelve chairs for the children who will hold up the letters. If the group is small, or space is limited, the letters could be hung or propped up by one child during the assembly. Plan where each character is to sit, and put a mark on the floor or mat for them.

Characters

Three kings, an innkeeper, stars, Mary and Joseph, angels, shepherds, a child in a party dress, an ox, holly, carol singers.

Costume suggestions

Stars: Make a simple shift from a rectangular strip of white material. Cut two holes for the arms, gather at the neck with elastic, hem the bottom, and trim the shift with tinsel.
Holly: Green or brown jumper and tights, with a crown of paper holly leaves and shiny red paper berries.
Ox: Keep this simple! Brown tights and jumper, with a pair of horns on a headband.

The performance

Make up a few appropriate sentences or a short verse about each of the themes below. To begin the assembly, play the introductory music. Then an adult or older child can read out the appropriate lines as the children play their parts.

C is for carols. The carol singers walk in singing, and sit in a group.

H is for holly. The child dressed as Holly brings in a holly bough to hang up, and then sits down.

R is for royal. The three kings walk in and sit in their places.

I is for inn. Switch on the light behind the inn door. The innkeeper opens the door and calls, 'No room, no room!'

S is for stars. After the reading, the stars dance on singing 'Twinkle twinkle little star'.

T is for tree. A child in a party dress brings a present to hang on the tree.

M is for Mary. Mary and Joseph walk in and gently place the baby in the manger. All sing 'Away in a Manger'.

A is for angels. The angels walk softly in and stand in position. You could have some quiet piano, recorder or guitar music here.

S is for shepherds. The shepherds walk in, and everyone sings 'While Shepherds Watched'.

J is for Jesus. Mary lifts the baby from the manger and holds him on her lap.

O is for ox. The ox walks slowly in and kneels beside the manger.

Y is for Yuletide. Hold up all the letters to spell out CHRISTMAS JOY.

Everybody then sings 'We wish you a merry Christmas'. Play some quiet music as the children walk out.

This suggested format gives you just the bare bones of the assembly. Flesh them out with carols, rhymes and prayers if you wish, but bear in mind that with small children it is best to keep the assembly fairly short.

The nativity story

What you need

A book which retells the Christmas story, such as *Away in a Manger* by Sarah Hayes, published by Walker Books, or *Long Ago in Bethlehem* by Masahiro Kasuya, published by A&C Black. (This is now out of print, but may still be available from the library.)

What to do

Any good retelling of the Christmas story can make an excellent basis for a Christmas assembly with children of about five or six.

Choose children to act each of the main parts. If they wish, let them speak any dialogue which is included in the book. You or another adult could read the narrative.

If you use *Away in a Manger*, you may like to sing the carols which are woven into the story. You could also add some appropriate carols to a reading of *Long Ago in Bethlehem*. It can be effective to have some quiet background music playing during the narration.

The number of carols and additional pieces you include will obviously depend upon the age and concentration span of the children involved, as well as the amount of time you have available. This sort of format is very flexible, however, and adapts well to most circumstances.

Bringing a gift

What you need
A collection of toys donated by the children — all in good condition. Invite a representative of a local children's home or hospital to receive the gifts.

What to do
This assembly is intended to encourage the children to think of giving as well as getting at Christmas. A local hospital or children's home could benefit from the gifts.

   The assembly is very easy to plan. Ask the children to bring a gift each, and come up during the assembly to place it at the foot of the Christmas tree. Sing some carols and Christmas songs. A Christmas crib makes a good addition to this occasion.

'The Pig and the Pudding'

Characters
Old woman, pig, cat, sheep, dog, mouse.

Props
Plastic bowl, jug, wooden spoon, table, improvised cooker top or home corner cooker, branches of holly. Make a simple doorway with a piece of cardboard from a large box, or just pretend!

Costumes
The old woman could wear a long dress and a shawl. Make some ears for the pig from pink card, and a curly tail, and cut out some appropriately shaped ears for the other animals, with whiskers for the cat and mouse. Dress the animals in appropriately coloured jumpers and tights.

What to do
Read the story aloud while the children act out the parts. They can speak the words written in inverted commas.

Once there was an old woman called Mrs Minch, who lived all by herself in a little house near a big wood. One cold December day she decided to make a Christmas pudding. She stirred together all the delicious ingredients, and put the pudding on the cooker to boil.
　'What a lovely Christmas pudding that will be,' said Mrs Minch to herself.
And it was a lovely pudding.
　A few hours later the pudding was cooked, and it smelled quite delicious. Mrs Minch left it on the table to cool, and went out to pick some holly branches to decorate her house for Christmas.
　No sooner had she gone than a pig came by. He sniffed the pudding.
　'Oink, oink! That smells delicious!'

He pushed open the door, went into the kitchen and gobbled up the pudding.

When Mrs Minch returned with her arms full of holly, she had quite a surprise! The pudding was gone — and she couldn't get back into her kitchen! The pig was so full of Christmas pudding that he couldn't move, and he was jammed in the doorway. Mrs Minch couldn't budge him, and he was too huge for her to step over. It was far too cold for Mrs Minch to stay outside for long. She sat down on the doorstep and cried.

'Miaow, miaow!'

At that moment a cat came by. He saw Mrs Minch crying, and stopped.

'What's the matter, Mrs Minch?' asked the cat.

'There's a pig in my kitchen and he's eaten my pudding, and now I can't get in!'

'Never mind — I'll shift him.'

The cat went over to the pig and tapped on his big pink belly — tap, tap!

'Who's that?' asked the pig.

'It's Mr Cat; I'll get you out. Let's see what all this fuss is about. You're as heavy as stone and sticky as jelly with all that pudding in your belly!'

And the cat pushed and pulled the pig, but he couldn't make him budge. So he went sadly away, leaving Mrs Minch on her doorstep, crying.

'Baa, baa!'

At that moment, a sheep came by. She saw Mrs Minch crying, and stopped.

'What's the matter, Mrs Minch?' asked the sheep.

'There's a pig in my kitchen and he's eaten my pudding, and now I can't get in!'

'Never mind — I'll shift him.'

The sheep went over to the pig and tapped on his big pink belly — tap, tap, tap!

'Who's that?' asked the pig.

'It's Mrs Sheep; I'll get you out. Let's see what all this fuss is about. You're as heavy as stone and sticky as jelly with all that pudding in your belly!'

And the sheep pushed and pulled the pig, but she couldn't make him budge. So she went sadly away, leaving Mrs Minch on her doorstep, crying.

'Woof, woof!'

At that moment a dog came by. He saw Mrs Minch crying, and stopped.

'What's the matter, Mrs Minch?' asked the dog.

'There's a pig in my kitchen and he's eaten my pudding, and now I can't get in!'

'Never mind — I'll shift him.'

The dog went over to the pig and tapped on his big pink belly — tap, tap, tap, tap!

'Who's that?' asked the pig.

'It's Mr Dog; I'll get you out. Let's see what all this fuss is about. You're as heavy as stone and sticky as jelly with all that pudding in your belly!'

And the dog pushed and pulled the pig, but he couldn't make him budge. So he went sadly away, leaving Mrs Minch on her doorstep, crying.

'Squeak, squeak!'

At that moment, a mouse came by. She saw Mrs Minch crying, and stopped.

'What's the matter, Mrs Minch?' asked the mouse.

'There's a pig in my kitchen and he's eaten my pudding, and now I can't get in!'

'Never mind — I'll shift him. Can I have a piece of your holly, please?'

The mouse went over to the pig and tapped on his big pink belly — tap, tap, tap, tap, tap!

'Who's that?' asked the pig.

'It's Mrs Mouse; I'll get you out. Let's see what all this fuss is about. Just hold your breath and shut your eyes, and I'll give you a big surprise!'

With that, the little mouse scuttled up to the pig and pricked him lightly with the holly, right on the tenderest part of his

belly. The pig was so surprised that he jumped right up in the air and wobbled off down the road as fast as he could go.

Mrs Minch was so pleased with the mouse that she offered her a cosy nest in the warmest part of the house. Later that day Mrs Minch made another Christmas pudding, and you can be sure that, when it was ready, the little mouse had as much Christmas pudding as she could eat!

Notes

Read the story to the children frequently, so that they become familiar with it. They will naturally start to join in with the words, so that by the time serious practice starts almost anyone will be able to take on any part! There will be many opportunities for talking about feeling sad, confident, disappointed or happy, and this will help the children as they act.

The children will enjoy the way the number of taps slowly increases. Ask someone in the wings to make the tapping noises with a piece of wood, and add some sound effects to represent the different animals coming up the road and going sadly away.

Christmas books

Chapter eight

The following list of books is a useful selection to choose from when planning your Christmas activities. For some of the books there are also suggestions for related activities.

These books and activities can help keep the children happily occupied during the busy run-up to Christmas.

The activities suggested in this chapter are intended as starting points for you to use and adapt as you wish. You may find that similar ideas can be adapted to suit other books which the children already know and enjoy.

All the stories are fun to read aloud and share with children, so relax and enjoy them!

Christmas story books

Thomas and the Missing Christmas Tree Christopher Awdry (Kaye & Ward)
The Bears' Christmas Stan and Jan Berenstain (Collins)
Christmas Alan Blackwood (Wayland)
Christmas Cat Peggy Blakeley (A&C Black)
The Smallest Christmas Tree Peggy Blakeley (A&C Black)
Winter Bear Ruth Craft and Eric Blegvad (Collins/Armada)
The Christmas Pageant Tomie de Paola (Methuen/Armada)
Away in a Manger Sarah Hayes (Walker Books)
Spot's First Christmas Eric Hill (Heinemann/Puffin)
Arthur's Christmas Cookies Lillian Hoban (World's Work)
The Silver Christmas Tree Pat Hutchins (Bodley Head)
Lucy and Tom's Christmas Shirley Hughes (Gollancz/Puffin)
Five Little Foxes and the Snow Tony Johnston and Cyndy Szekeres (World's Work)
Long Ago in Bethlehem Masahiro Kasuya (A&C Black)
Mog's Christmas Judith Kerr (Collins/Armada)

Winter Bear

An interesting follow-up to this story could be a topic about warm clothes for winter.
● Ask the children to collect pictures of winter clothing from catalogues.
● Talk about materials which keep us dry, warm or cool, and collect some examples.

Spot's First Christmas

What you need
Card, coloured and plain paper, scissors.

What to do
• Using stiff card, make some templates in the shapes of Spot's presents. Ask the children to draw round the templates and cut out the shapes. Then mount them on sugar paper. Can their parents or friends guess what the parcels are?
• Play a memory game with Spot's presents, covering them up and then seeing how many the children can remember.

Arthur's Christmas Cookies

This story could be used after a session of cooking.
• Ask the children to compare the ingredients and talk about the results. Collect pictures of food.
• Organise a tasting of sweets, peanuts, sweet and savoury biscuits and so on. This is both interesting and fun!

Lucy and Tom's Christmas

Try the following activities:
• Collect some presents together and play the memory game. Spread the objects on the floor and count them. Cover them with a cloth, and see how many the children can remember. Take one away, and ask which is missing.
• Make cut out pictures of Lucy and Tom's family, and mount them on card. Use them to help match the presents to their owners. Ask how many people

there are in the family, and
how many presents there are.

The Silver Christmas Tree

What you need
Tree branches, fir cones, string, Plasticine,
frieze paper, silver paper.

What to do
Make a little tree by tying together
several bare branches. Use a tub of
Plasticine as a base. Put a piece of dark
blue frieze paper behind the tree. Make
a silver paper star to stick on the paper
above the tree.

Five Little Foxes and the Snow

- After reading the story, ask the
children to collect some things which
come in pairs, such as socks, slippers,
ballet shoes, gloves and mittens.
- Mix all the objects up, and ask the
children to match the pairs.

Mog's Christmas

- After reading the story, talk about
family gatherings and relations. Ask the
children to draw their family. Do they live
nearby? Do they come to stay?
- Discuss special family occasions such
as weddings, birthdays and holidays.

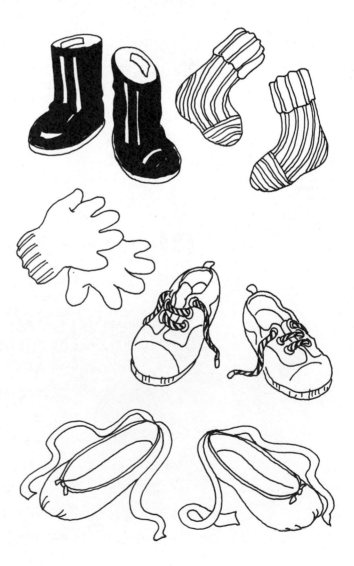

Photocopiable material

Chapter nine

Use worksheets to provide the children with a quiet and purposeful activity when they want one. If the worksheets on pages 84 to 90 are carefully introduced, they can be used at will by the children during the busy days before Christmas.

Each sheet requires a certain amount of thought and observation, as well as pencil and scissor control.

The sheets can be photocopied and adapted as you wish, to suit the age and ability of your children. Follow up the worksheet activities by talking about them with the children.

Dot-to-dot snowman

Join the dots.
Draw the face.
Draw lots of tiny
snowflakes.
Colour the scarf and hat.

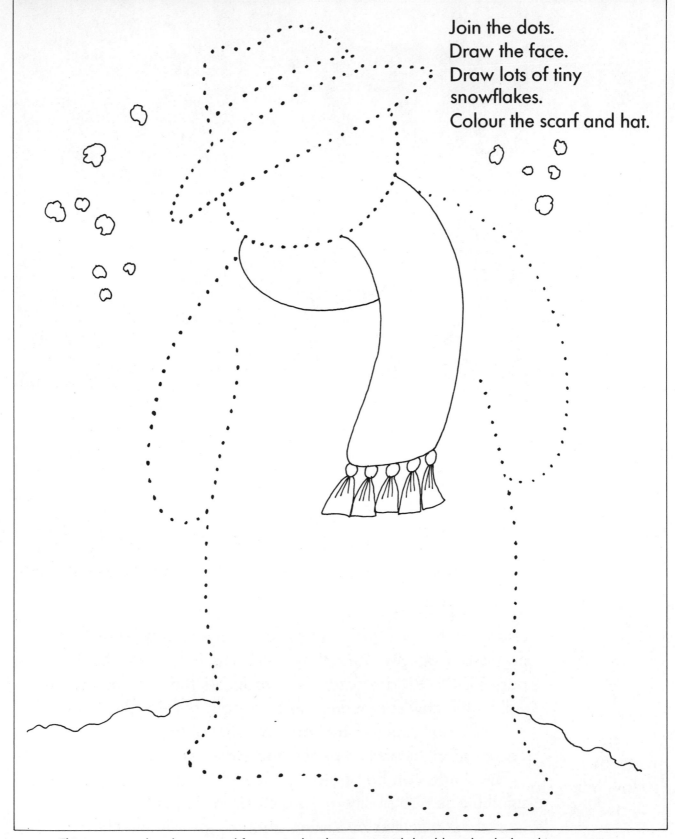

Star shapes

Join the dots.
Colour the stars.
Cut them out and mount them.
How many stars?
Draw the number.

Joining the pictures

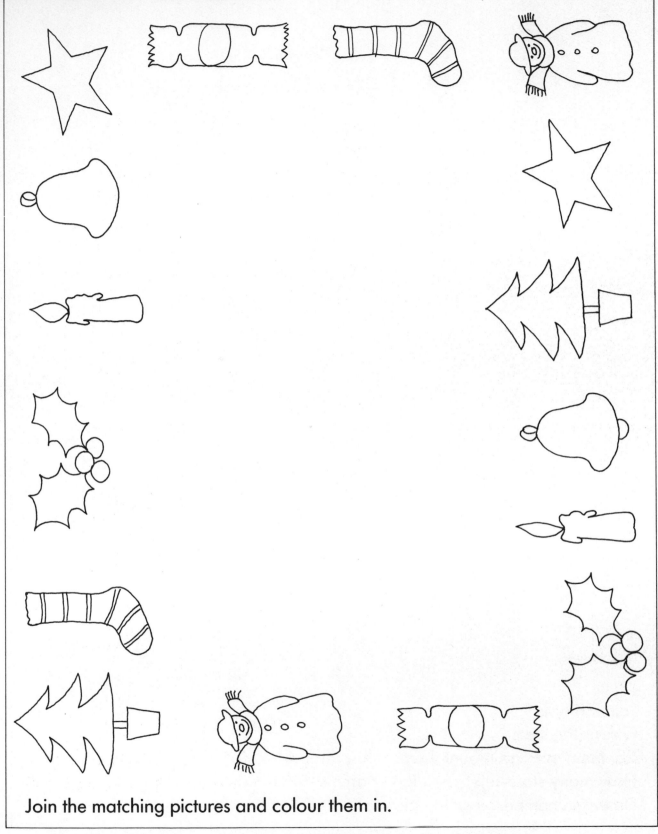

Join the matching pictures and colour them in.

Christmas tree

Talk about the tree. Have you a tree at home? Is it a living tree? How many candles can you see? How many parcels? What could be in the round parcel? Join the dots and colour the picture.

Party balloons

Join the dots. Draw strings to the girl's hand. Colour the balloons. How many balloons are there? How many round ones? How many long ones?

Finish the parcels

Complete the parcels and colour them in.

Candles

Join the dots. Colour the candles. How many are there? What happens to a candle when it burns? Which is the tallest candle? Which is the smallest?

Cut-out snowmen, see page 20

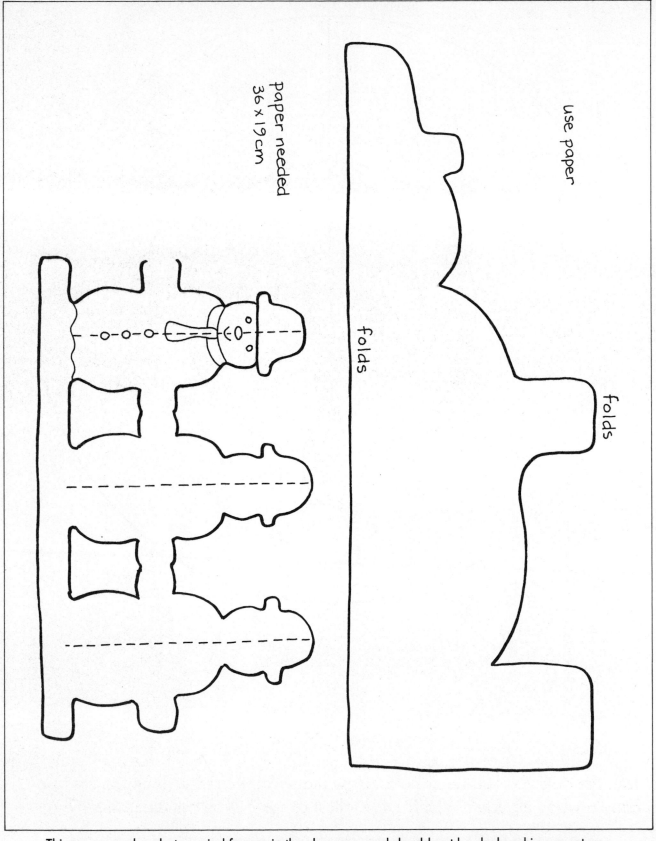

paper needed
36 x 19 cm

use paper

folds

folds

Tree-top fairy or angel, see page 24

cut out

wings

arms

Robins and tiny robins, see pages 41 and 25

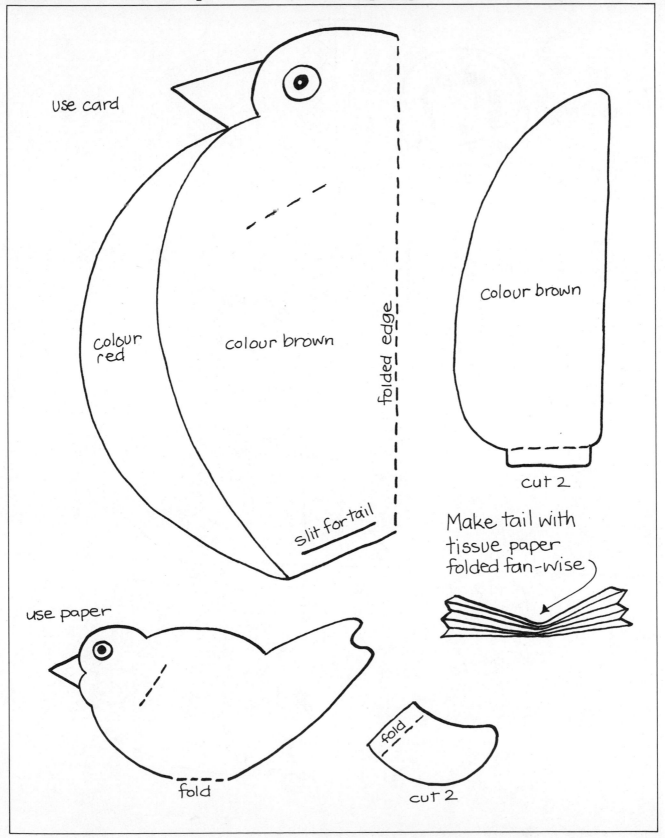

use card

colour red

colour brown

folded edge

slit for tail

colour brown

cut 2

Make tail with tissue paper folded fan-wise

use paper

fold

fold

cut 2

Lavender lady, see page 28

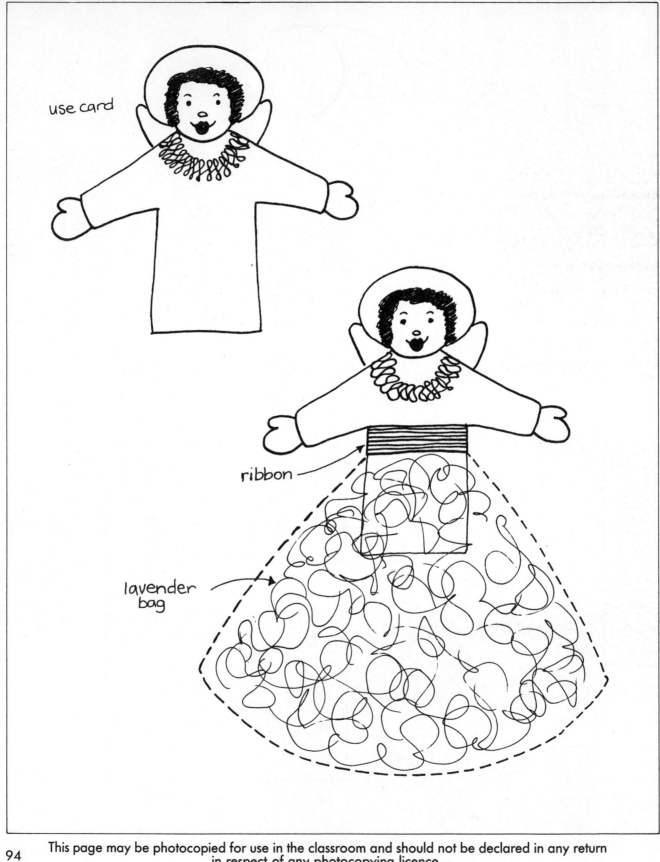

use card

ribbon

lavender
bag

This page may be photocopied for use in the classroom and should not be declared in any return
in respect of any photocopying licence.

'Dickory Dock' bookmark, see page 30

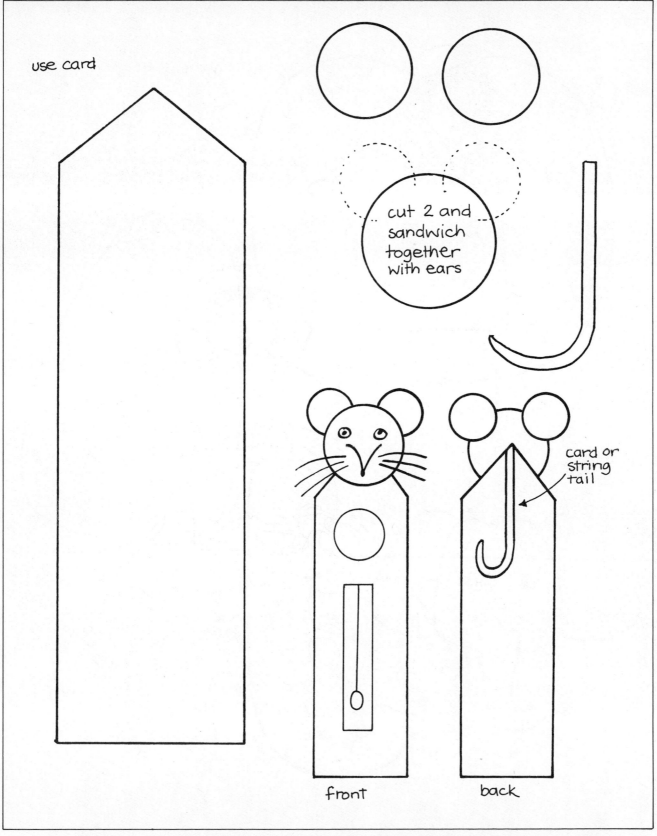

use card

cut 2 and sandwich together with ears

card or string tail

front

back

Reminder board, see page 32

use sugar paper

head

ears

assembly

trunk

This page may be photocopied for use in the classroom and should not be declared in any return
in respect of any photocopying licence.